THE STING OF REJECTION

From Pain to Purpose

Rosita Pinder

ISBN: 978-976-97183-0-2

Editing / Book Layout by

Passionate Words Editing Services

(IG @passionate.words.editing246)

ACKNOWLEDGEMENTS

I want thank God for his Holy Spirit, who has filled my heart and thoughts with these inspiring downloads of wisdom and knowledge to be able to share with you.

I want to thank Apostle Samson Yakubu who has been instrumental in offering his invaluable inputs into this material. I want to also thank Apostle Paul Fearon for his time, input and support.

I want to thank Sis. Watson who has now gone on to be with the Lord, for seeing the book in me and for her love, prayers, encouragement and Godly advice. I thank her Widower Daddy Watson, who has always been an encourager and a pillar of strength.

I want to recognize the love and support from family and friends and everyone who has walked with me along this journey for bringing this thought into reality.

FOREWORD

In life we ask so many questions that we ourselves are not able to comprehend. Sometimes you will have ups and you will definitely have downs; the one thing that brings hope is the knowledge of the word of God. He has promised to work his purposes out in our lives even in the midst of our pain. It is the painful process that births forth purpose in life, which leads us to our destiny. Like me, you probably have experienced rejection and many pains in life, when you thought all hope was gone. But then he touches you, and ignites his love that surpasses your finite conclusions on your life. In essence, keep faith alive and keep believing that everything you have been through is not for you but to help others along their journey.

THANK YOU

I am grateful to our Lord and Saviour Jesus Christ, the Author and finisher of our faith, for entrusting me with words of wisdom and knowledge to encourage you and to let you know that you are loved by God. I am grateful for the true friends Jehovah God has placed in my life that saw the potential in me to write this book.

Thank you for taking the time out to read this book, I hope it will be of tremendous help to you. Share what was shared with you to others around you as we spread the love and joy of God. May God grant you the peace, joy and deliverance you desire, as you overcome the dreaded spirit of rejection to accomplish his will in your life.

TABLE OF CONTENTS

INTRODUCTION

In the journey of life many people have been victims of the vicious cycle of rejection: not fully understanding its causes in their lives, emotions and physiological makeup, its effects on their thought process and the pain that it brings. Oftentimes it can drive people in the direction of doing something they don't want to because of ego, poor self-image and weakened self-esteem. These three components make up a recipe for disaster in many lives, and their effects can be trans-generational if not nipped in the bud. This book is intended to identify the pain and effects of rejection and how to recover from its stigma, its trauma and to prevent its re-occurrence in a lifetime. Everyone experiences rejection at varying degrees, depending on their unique backgrounds, exposure, experiences, and innate purpose. However, once you have overcome it, you will realize new levels of joy and fulfilment! Walk through the process and you will see the beautiful artistry God has intended for your life. Stay with me as we explore the dynamics of rejection and embrace the joy, acceptance and relevance towards living a fulfilling life.

CHAPTER ONE:
Rejection Defined

In an effort to fully understand the concept of rejection, it is good to set the tone for defining what rejection is, which means 'refusing to take; denial; cast away or to discard' – this is according to the New Webster's Dictionary. Based on this fact, I believe that many people can relate to instances where they were refused an opportunity that could have resulted in great success in their lives at some point. Also, I am sure that you can relate to instances where you were, for reasons unknown to you, cast away or discarded. Although persons can have the relevant qualifications, talents and gifts to do an exceptional job, they can still be denied the chance to showcase their ability to make a difference in the lives of others. This could also be the result of rejection.

I believe that many have experience this scenario at some point in their lives – in some cases, repeatedly. Rejection can come at any point in our lives and for any reason. However, in most cases, it could mean the timing could have been off, or it could be that God in his love was shielding them from making the wrong decision in the long run.

There are many instances where rejection could be experienced in a person's life, either consciously or subconsciously. This may affect their emotions and outlook on life. This could also affect how they view themselves and how they, in turn, treat other people in a similar manner. Some may argue that being rejected is a normal part of life and human development. However, this may not necessarily be the case, because the essence of this work is to open the minds of people to do some introspection in order to arrive at a reasonable conclusion in finding ways to mitigate this dilemma. This knowledge gives us an idea that can allow us to make better decisions and to avoid the narrative of self sabotage to allow us to succeed in life.

In some ways, rejection can bring some benefits if persons pay close enough attention to understanding the different dynamics of the root cause and ways to mitigate its impact. Consequently, the experience will cause persons to learn, grow and understand how to navigate the impact of rejection.

Once this happens, the person is in a good position to pass on valuable knowledge to help others along their voyage. Chapter Two looks closely at the place of rejection and what it means in your life and circumstances.

CHAPTER TWO:
The Types of Rejection

When we think of rejection, we think of just being refused, but they are two main types of rejection. This chapter seeks to identify and explain them so that we can have a better understanding of when these occur in our lives.

Unspoken

his occurs when someone deliberately refuses to respond to you as you try to reach out to them. This can be in the form of not answering or returning your messages or calls; refusing to acknowledge someone's presence or their attempt to speak to you face-to-face. Thank God that he is not like this and is always there to listen to and answer us when we call on him. Isaiah 65: 24 (NIV) makes this clear when he says *"Before they call I will answer; while they are still speaking I will hear."* This gives us the assurance that God is more willing to answer us than we can call on him. I am sure this kind and caring character makes us feel accepted and loved. Having the understanding that a great wonderful God has more than enough time to hear and answer us from his heart can truly boost one's self esteem.

Spoken

This occurs when someone makes utterances that make it clear that they, for various reasons, do not accept you in their life. The good thing about this type of rejection is that it is easy to know and to bring closure to the situation because it has been said. This, as harsh as it is, brings comfort and puts you in a position of knowing where you stand with a particular person or group. In some cases, for instance, *"I do not want you in my life."* Yes, it will hurt you because you are human and your desire is to be accepted and loved like anyone else would like to be. Jesus said that who comes to him he will not cast away. This hope brings the joy needed to feel a sense of acceptance, which in turn boosts self worth. Probably at some point in life we were told that we were not good enough or that we are not the one wanted or required. These words can have a lasting impact on our lives because of the roots they have planted within us.

Words are very powerful and can make or break us if we allow them to penetrate our emotions. God, in Genesis Chapter 1, created the world and every living creature with words. When a word, whether good or bad, is released, it has the power to manifest and bring forth what was said. God said, "Let there be light," and there was light. It immediately happens once the word is spoken. Similarly, this occurs when negative words of rejection are spoken over our lives. The good thing about this is that we have the authority to cancel every negative word spoken over our lives so that it will not take root and grow.

What Is Spoken Vs. What Is Seen

Many studies have proven that body language is the most accurate form of communication in comparison to what is said. This is a fact — and many people also believe that actions speak louder than words. What is done to and how we treat people is felt and, in most cases, noticed by the victim.

The impact of words, however, can be very detrimental to the hearer it is intended for, especially if they are negative. The bible reminds us in Colossians 4:6 (KJV) to *"[l]et your speech be alway with grace, seasoned with salt, that ye may know how ye ought to answer every man."* How we converse with someone can have many negative implications on their emotions and can damage their self-esteem. What does salt do? It adds flavour to the pot and without it the food will be tasteless. As children of God we ought to examine the words that are coming out of our mouths, as they can ensnare someone and cause them to be a failure.

Our words and our Father Jesus Christ's words should be the same because he is gracious, forgiving and caring towards his precious creation. What will you do? Try to understand people instead of pushing them away because they do not measure up to your standards. Everyone we meet is fighting an internal battle; if you took the time to give them the opportunity to share their story, your attitude towards them would most likely take a spin in a positive direction. Love covers a multitude of sins, so be nice to everyone you meet and this is one sure way of doing the will of our Heavenly Father.

Prayer: *I renounce every negative word rather spoken or unspoken, self imposed or spoken by others from over my life; I pull them down and trample under feet every contrary word that is not in alignment with your word and I decree and declare that I am accepted by Jesus and he has good plans in store for my life. In Jesus' name. Amen. Feel free to do the actions as you are led while praying this prayer.*

Words have the ability to ignite positive or negative emotions within us, which are fed to our spirits and souls consciously or unconsciously. This is important, when words are spoken towards or over us. God has given us the authority to cancel and reject these words from taking effect in our lives. Cheer up, all is not lost, Jesus has come to set the captives free. Take a moment to reflect on your life to identify any patterns or cycles that you seem not to be able to break free from.

This can be the result of a negative word spoken over your life that has taken root and now the fruits are imminent due to the outcomes in your life.

I remember doing a Psychology class as part of my university degree. The class taught me that there is a term called "Self-Fulfilling Prophecy", which means that as something is repeated to us for a while, we begin to believe what was said. This then becomes a part of us and we become that which was spoken.

Self Fulfilling Prophecy
(Pygmalion Effect)

The above diagram shows the cycle of the Self-Fulfilling Prophecy and how it can give birth to what we believe. Our mind is a powerhouse that holds our beliefs and builds our confidence by allowing us to pursue what we believe we can do; it also gives momentum to others to fulfil their dreams. The major Jericho wall to overcome here is what we believe; which are the negative reinforcements about self and life. What we believe about ourselves and our abilities can influence our actions towards others because of the seeds which were planted in our minds. This then impacts other's beliefs about us and it causes other's actions towards us to be influenced. This process reinforces our beliefs about ourselves. This cycle will continue to be renewed until it is broken by positive reinforcement and believes about ourselves.

Our thoughts can keep us captive and from reaching out to others who have the tools to help us but instead we remain captive to our negative thought patterns. This then impacts the beliefs and actions of others towards us, as they can see our behaviours and respond to them in the same manner. For instance, if you are of the belief that you will never be accepted by people, your actions show this and it can cause others to refrain from being around you. Then these actions qualify people's beliefs of us, which can be seen by the way we are acting. The below illustration explains the self-fulfilling prophecy in more detail.

Beliefs → Actions = Self-fulfilling Prophecy

Your beliefs about yourself play a vital role in how you perceive yourself, which leads to actions that depict these beliefs. The bible reminds us in Proverbs 23:7 (NKJV) *"For as he thinks in his heart, so is he. "Eat and drink!" he says to you, But his heart is not with you"*. The genesis of this verse, *"For as he thinks in his heart…"* indicates that whatever flows from the heart takes up a big space in how we view our external realities, which then become who we are as a person and drives our actions. It is important to put yourself in an environment that would cause you to think positive thoughts, which will in turn make you a more positive person and your negative views about yourself begin to diminish bit by bit. Everything in life starts with a thought – what we accept as true from our mind.

This is where the true battle begins – our perceptions, actions and end results, begins and ends with the mind. ***The heart:*** The heart is known as an organ that pumps blood throughout the body and is at the centre of our circulatory system. This vessel is used to transmit oxygen to every cell; in essence it is the powerhouse that sends life to what we nourish which is transmitted to our minds then back to our heart, as the two work hand in hand as a result, giving oxygen, which represents life, to what we believe. The heart is the engine that makes friends with its neighbour oxygen who then makes friends with the mind; this is how the prophecy about self is orchestrated and then fulfilled.

The two below scenarios are typical examples of self-fulfilling prophecy, as follows:

Scenario One:

Theresa always believed from childhood that she would never be successful in life based on what her parents told her, *"You will never be anything in life."* Because this was said by the authorities over her life, her parents, it created an avenue for the enemy to plant seeds of despair. She accepted what was said and never became anything substantial in her life.

Scenario Two:

Remino believed that one day he will become a pilot. He reinforced this belief when asked what he wanted to be when he grew up – and today he is a pilot. His parents were always speaking positive words into his life and encouraging him to achieve his goals, which made his journey easier to accomplish. Hebrews 11:1 (KJV), *"Now faith is the substance of things hoped for, the evidence of things not seen."* Faith causes us to believe by taking action, as faith without works is dead. Even though it was futuristic he had a focus point and positive words that were being formed around him to bring it to pass.

Thank God for the Deliverance Ministry which affords us the assistance we need to get the type of intervention necessary to overcome these obstacles. Jesus said, in St. John 11:43 (KJV), *"And when he thus had spoken, he cried with a loud voice, Lazarus, come forth."* Our words give life to what we thought was dead and impossible to live. This takes faith in believing that God is who he said he is and we can create life to our circumstances.

The question is: Whose words will you believe?

Our spirit has a voice that speaks from our innermost being. It is that voice that influences our emotions and guides our actions. The voice of God through his Holy Spirit speaks to us concerning all aspects of our lives: what we should or should not do, the direction we should or should not take. He answers questions we oftentimes have and he gives us the truth and the best advice we could ever imagine receiving into our lives. It may not be what we want to hear – sweet candy-cane words that will give us a high but then we are still stranded in the same position doing nothing and going nowhere. It is the words of the Holy Spirit that challenge us to take a long deep look at ourselves in the mirror and compel us to make the necessary changes that will take us into our land of prosperity.

This prosperity can manifest in many forms, it can come in the form of freedom from what had you bound; peace of mind, a joyful heart, making a Godly decision and walking out your God-ordained life. This brings happiness, and fulfilment that nothing in this world could ever measure up to or replace. It is a settled outcome which God has promised those who follow his precepts and walk in his ways. Is it easy? No. Is the process smooth? No. Here comes the *'BUT'*, it will be worth it in the end. It is the going through that causes us not to see the end result of what God is doing. Our pain is bigger than us and will touch many lives, we are often times unaware of it until it actually happens. God leads us beside the still waters and restores our soul to a place where we are glad, where we are full and ready to pour out to others we come into contact within our day-to-day lives as we go through the process of hurt, pain, rejection, anxiety, doubt, fear and the list can go on until we come to the realisation that God's way is the best way. Stay the course, God is painting a beautiful picture that many will be amazed at and in owe to gaze upon. The **B.U.T.** below encapsulates the formula we need for guaranteed success.

The **B – Bravery:** It will take something you have never done to get what you have never had. It's good to have faith, then to put this faith into action through believing, but it is great when we can step out when the odds are looking us in the face, then to look them back in the face and put into action what we once believed.

The **U – The Unrelenting**: In the doing, this is when we determine in our minds that greater is he who is within us than he who is in the world. When we pull out those memory verses from Sunday School, reminding ourselves that we can do all things through Christ who strengthens us. Not giving in when you are weak and weary, but fighting the good fight of faith and pressing through the crowd like the woman with the issue of blood until she achieved her ultimate goal of being healed.

The **T** – The **Triumph**: When you continue to make progress in your life, gradually success will be around the corner. You can feel it coming, as the major obstacles become minute in your eyes, small enough to be trampled on. This final stage can only come when we have overcome the **B** and **U**, then it is easy to come into the place of Triumph.

God speaks to us because he wants to lead us to a destination of success. The devil also speaks to us, opposing everything that God says to us that will bring about success. His words kill what God wants to do in our lives – imagine pouring a poisonous substance on a plant. The obvious is true, it will eventually die; this is not the promise of God for us, as he promises us life and in abundance. St. John 10:10 (KJV) reminds us, that *"The thief cometh not, but for to steal, and to kill, and to destroy: I am come that they might have life, and that they might have it more abundantly."* The words of God are spirit and they are life. Jesus is the living word, when he speaks, he speaks life into our circumstances, when it seems like nothing can be done. When we have exhausted our human capabilities, when our finite minds cannot comprehend it all, this is when God steps in. St. John 6:63 (NLT) says, *"The Spirit alone gives eternal life. Human effort accomplishes nothing. And the very words I have spoken to you are spirit and life"*.

How Do We Differentiate the Voice of God Vs. The Voice of the Devil?

There is always a peace that comes when God speaks to us. He is sovereign and he can speak to us as he desires, which can come in many forms. He can use people in authority to speak to us; Christians or ordinary people, his word, songs, poems or anything in the present moment to comfort us, to teach us something or to warn us away from doing something that will be detrimental to us or our loved ones. His utterances are always in alignment with his word the bible. What are you hearing? Is it in the bible? Does it bear witness with his word? If you are not sure, take it to God in prayer. He will bring the confirmation you need to make the next step. Making the wrong move can cause you years of walking around in the wilderness not knowing where you are going and when you will arrive, just like the children wondering around in the wilderness for forty years, because of one wrong move that Moses took. Looking at the bigger picture, our wrong moves are tied to the destinies of many people whom we are connected to.

I have always believed that everyone in our lives is there for a reason. It is our duty to find out why and to not allow ourselves to be a hindrance to the destiny of the people whom God has sent into our lives. Sounds like a big task, but it can be simplified if we ask God to show us the reasons why the people who are in our lives at any given time are there. There is a reason for everything, our God is a purposeful God and we ought to be too, as we are created in his image. The devil uses his demons and people whom he influences or people who are possessed with demons to attempt to make us doubt what God is saying, or even challenge what God has said so that we will disobey him and go in the wrong direction. The story of Adam and Eve in the garden of Eden is a perfect example, where the snake, which represents the devil, questioned the word of God and created doubt and unbelief in the heart of Eve, as a strategy to get her to disobey the commands of God and do what he wanted her to do, which was to eat from the forbidden tree. This cost them their relationship with God and a perfect life, where everything was provided for them. They were stripped of their rights and authority, which has caused all of humanity to be in agony. This brings to light the importance of knowing what the bible says and not allowing the devil to tempt us to divert from it because they are consequences for our actions. The devil will never tell you to do anything that is godly because he is an enemy of God, which means he is our enemy too. He opposes everything God says to do, as well as his word. When we disobey the word of God, this brings regret, disappointment, pain and bondage into our lives. The devil will never tell us to do what God, has said.

The devil is very clever. The bible says that he can transform himself like an Angel of light, so be always on your guard. If you hear a voice speaking and you are not sure, remember to always take it to God in prayer, seek godly counsel from your Pastor, Elders, Leaders or a mature Christian friend or a Christian Counsellor. We are no match for the devil, so use the resources God has given you and God will reveal his truth when you seek for it. He said he will never leave us nor forsake us; his presence is always with us. I know at times it may seem like he has forsaken you, especially at a time you thought he would be there for you. People who you thought were close to you abandoned you, but be assured that you are never alone. Spend time in the presence of God daily to practice listening to his voice, so that you will know it when you hear it. Automatically, you will develop a love for his word as well, because he is the Living Word. We learn of his character, his personality and his nature. Having these weapons will give you a greater chance of differentiating his voice from the enemy's voice.

CHAPTER THREE:
The Place of Rejection

Everyone is born with an innate ability to love and be loved, but circumstances – in some cases beyond our control (for instance, having experienced abuse, whether verbally or physically by parents, being raped as a child, being rejected by parents, or being adopted) – can have serious implications into one's adult life. These negative experiences are like glue that sticks to our emotions until we get the help we need to break the invisible chains that can hold us bound for as long as a lifetime. It can be a very lonely and sad place to be. What makes it worse is not having the support needed to overcome this daunting period in your life. God says in his Word, Luke 4:18 (NLT), "The Spirit of the Lord is upon me, for he has anointed me to bring Good News to the poor. He has sent me to proclaim that captives will be released, that the blind will see, that the oppressed will be set free". *This means* that he has come to set us free, which signifies that he wants us to live a life of joy, hope and happiness, which truly can only be found in him. In search for this hope and happiness, we can resort to drugs, ungodly relationships, sex, partying or overeating just to name a few of the things that we seek to cling onto for comfort emotionally.

How do we know that rejection is affecting us? Take a look at the below illustration, which shows the linkage of the (RSAS) syndrome: Rejection, Self-blame, Anger and Sorrow.

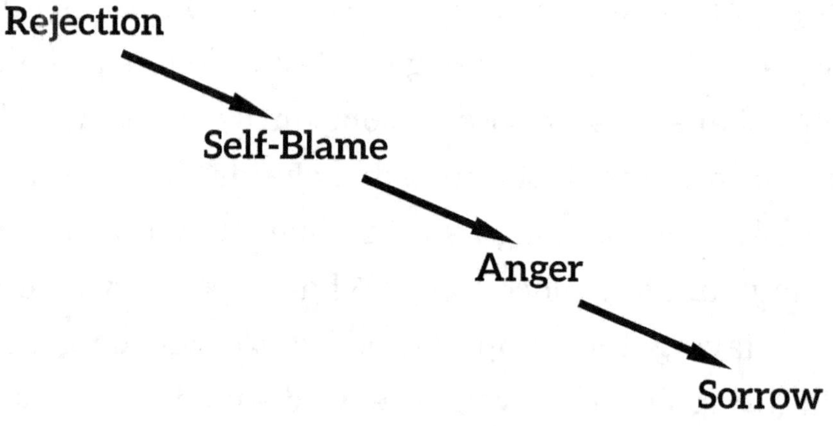

Rejection outside of God's purpose for our life's destiny is not a blessing, but a curse. Why do I say that? In terms of experiencing **rejection**, first of all, it is not pleasant. This can lead you on a downward slope with feelings of **self-blame**, believing that it was your fault that caused you to be rejected or that you are not good enough to come up to the standards of others. This then leads you on a further downward slope towards **anger**. Feelings of anger are developed because of the constant occurrence of being rejected. Imagine wanting to express your true acceptance of someone but instead they keep dismissing you, resulting in a breakdown of relationship, causing you to lose that person. This then leads to feelings of **sorrow**, which is a feeling of immense distress caused by loss. This loss could signify anything or anyone of value to us, which we no longer have around. Sorrow is more intense when compared to **sadness**.

Once you are in a place where you have been rejected, either by parents, family members, classmates, work colleagues, church family or leaders, just be assured that God is in the midst of your circumstance working his purposes out behind the scenes. This was brought to light when Joseph was rejected by his brothers because of their jealousy towards him; he suffered pain and betrayal from whom he thought would have been happy and supportive of him. The opposite occurred and he was thrown into the pit and sold into Egypt. Little did they know that what they did to him was God's perfect plan for him to be trained to fulfil his destiny! There is no purpose if pain is not involved and there is no destiny if you did not take the trail that is marked rejection.

Rejection from the Closest Ones to You

Jesus suffered tremendous rejection from his own but yet he did not allow it to abort his destiny. Thank God he endured unto death because – guess what? We would be far more lost today, unforgiven and doomed for judgement. If God himself was rejected, what makes us believe that it would not happen to us, especially by those who are closest to us? The pain is greater from the ones whom we have trusted and poured out our deepest secrets to, which we would have only told to them, who then break our trust and cause pain that can last for many years – sometimes even a lifetime. The time of most pain, in my opinion, was when Jesus really needed his disciples to be there for him and for them to have stood up for him, but, rather, they denied him. The Bible gives us a perfect example of this occurrence in Luke 22:54-62. Even though it was clear that Peter was seen with Jesus, he decided to turn his back on him. I can recollect when I was in college and I was going through a break-up. I really wanted my good friend who went to school with me at secondary school and shared a good friendship to have been there for me. However, he just ran off and left me to face the emotional pain alone. Years after, I saw him and felt resentment toward him for not being there at the point of greatest need. This paints a clear picture of the pain rejection can cause you. It is like you have never known this person who is being rejected and that their life is not valuable in your sight.

Lonesome Road Ahead

Rejection in itself can push persons into isolation, which means that everyone discards the rejected person for one reason or the other. This can leave one feeling like rubbish; not a pleasant feeling at all. God has created us to be a part of a community, where we can be accepted and feel loved. The first such relationship was with Adam and his family back in the Garden of Eden, Gen 4:1-2. Relationships are very important to God and they should be to us as well, as we are social beings longing for companionship and approval of each other; a true sense of belonging to a group. The breakdown can come when someone feels like they are not a part of a unit or that they don't fit in with a particular group.

One can be a part of a family, not being outwardly rejected, but indirectly experiencing rejection because of their stance for Jesus when their family does not. This is a subtle way of being rejected by loved ones because of different beliefs. I found myself in this place years ago when I lived with my family, being present in the same space but yet not feeling a part of my family. I was always considered as the *"know it all"*, *"better than"* person.

However, Jesus promises us that he will never leave us nor forsake us. This is demonstrated in Deuteronomy 31:6 when Moses spoke to the Israelites; he commanded them to be strong and courageous with the assurance that God will never leave nor forsake them. The road will get lonesome but you will never experience loneliness because his presence is always with us, even to the end of time.

Self Pity

In order to have a better understanding of self pity, let's look at its definition before we proceed. What is self pity? It can be defined as a sense of feeling sorry for oneself. It is a place of feeling vulnerable to the situations that you are confronted with while looking down on yourself in a negative manner. For instance, internalising your situation as being exceedingly worse than others by saying, *"it's my fault"* and *"poor me"*, while expecting validation from others. This scenario paints a pretty good picture of how easily we can become prisoners to our own situations, looking through the narrow lens of obscurity. The good thing about this is that it does not have to be this way forever, change is possible. The bible reminds us in Colossians 3:2, NIV, *to "Set your mind on things above, not on earthly things"*. This can allow us to focus on God and the things that signify his character, such as his love and his compassion instead of what we are going through or have been through.

None of us are exempt from troubles and difficult situations; however, it is our reaction to these situations that makes us a victor or a victim. One of the interesting things about being a part of a sporting team is that whether your team wins or loses, everyone is still expected to shake the hands of the other team. This test proves our ability to quickly overcome feelings of defeat and that the ability to rise from the ashes with a positive attitude is possible. This creates a win-win situation that fosters the momentum to keep the fire burning amidst turmoil and the negative emotions that want to overtake you.

Chapter Four: Causes of Rejection

This chapter will look at some of the origins of rejection, which can come in many forms; this will allow you to understand why you have experienced rejection and in which form it came.

God Ordained

Everyone has been born for a purpose and we ourselves sometimes struggle to identify this reality. Some people are able to find their purpose early in life and some of us later. The mistake we often times make is to look at the lives of others and make a comparison to ours. Bear in mind that some people may have found it easy to accomplish their goals in life, while others have the humps, bumps and roller-coaster rides. This does not mean that anything is wrong with you; God knows what he is doing. Jeremiah 29:11 (NLT) reinforces this point. *"For I know the plans I have for you," says the Lord. "They are plans for good and not for disaster, to give you a future and a hope".*

The plans of God are good plans, which were ordained even before we were born, even before our parents knew our names, even before we were placed in the families we found ourselves in.

Sometimes God can cause us to go through a series of rejections from our families, friends, strangers, church families and work colleagues. Why is this? This seems to be a question many of us who have experienced rejection have asked at some point. God can allow you to go through rejection because he has a plan for your life that includes you going through this experience to teach you on an emotional level what it means to have walked this road to equip you for your journey ahead. All trees bear at different times during the year, under different climates and some bear faster than others. The *'key'* thing is that a tree bears its fruit in its season. When we are going through our seasons of rejection, it will bear fruit at the appointed time. This is to share with others our journey and how it can add value to the lives of those whom we come into contact with. Mark 12:10 (KJV) states, *"And have ye not read this scripture; The stone which the builders rejected is become the head of the corner:"* This scripture teaches us that the main person (in this case, Jesus) was rejected but it was needed in order to deliver us from many dangers ahead and, in most cases, from ourselves. What about David in 1 Samuel 16:11, who was forgotten by his father when Samuel was looking for him to anoint him King of Israel? When you have greatness on your life, God will orchestrate the right people to seek us out at the appointed time. It seemed like he was a nobody, going nowhere, just conditioned to tending sheep. Even though naturally this was true, God was preparing him spiritually for greatness, training him for the office he was about to be promoted to.

God works in ways we will never understand but in the end it will be for our good. It took skill and bravery for David to have killed a lion and a bear with his bare hands, but little did he know that this was preparing him for a particular purpose that God has chosen only for him to fulfil. "God is looking for you with the horn of oil in his hand." The two major questions are, "Are you in the right place?" and "Are you prepared?" God will not anoint an un-prepared person, as he is a God of excellence and structure. The Kingdom of God is filled with skilled, knowledgeable and prepared people. He wants us to look, act and be the part that he has called us to be; this includes being fully prepared.

Your Appearance

We as human beings tend to judge people just by a glance at their appearance and, if it is not to our personal satisfaction, that person is automatically rejected. Thank God that this is not so with him, for the bible warns us that man looks on the outward appearance but God looks at the heart. If we used the physical appearance to select a person for a particular task or even for acceptance, we would have missed many persons whom God has sent into our lives to be a blessing and to take us to the next level in our lives. It is imperative to get to know someone the way God does; this is to see people through the eyes of God in a non-judgemental way. True intentions of the heart are made up of our motives, which drive us in life, and these are proven in our actions that cannot be hidden.

I remember, earlier in my career, I would always avoid speaking to a lady because she, in my opinion, looked like a frog. I would pass judgements because of how she looked with scars on her skin. Later in life, however, I reflected on that situation and asked God to forgive me for how I viewed his creation. It taught me not to judge or look down on people because they might not be appealing to our eyes. All of us were created in the image of God, hand crafted by him, and there is nothing that he has made that was not good. In really getting to know her and understanding why the scars were on her skin, I overlooked her appearance and saw her as a loving daughter of God whom he dearly loves. I really felt her pain when she said she was assaulted and had an attempted rape, which resulted in her skin being scarred. This changed the way I related to and viewed people from that time onward. Sometimes situations like this one can confront us, in a challenging way, to change something about ourselves that can be a hindrance to us growing and having God ordained relationships.

God reminded Joshua to be courageous and Jeremiah not to be afraid of men and their faces. Sometimes the faces of people, if we allow it, can be intimidating, but once we are confident in the God we serve and in ourselves we will not fall prey to this strategy the devil uses to deter us from the path God wants us to walk. The physical appearance of people can also be deceitful: someone can smile when they are sad inside; someone can look angry on the outside but might be the nicest person you have ever met. This brings me to share an experience I had over ten years ago with a woman whom I called Mom, who seemed very unapproachable. I said to myself, "I will never talk to her!"; she seemed so serious and I was afraid of her. A few years after this encounter, I really needed someone to talk to about a situation I was going through and guess what? Yes, she was the only one at the time available and I needed urgent help. I remembered calling the moderator of a Christian broadcast and the Pastor said, "I know someone who does counselling." I called the number that the Pastor gave me and, to my surprise, it was her. I was speechless and ashamed of myself to know that the perception which I had formed of her was not a reality. She was able to listen to my concerns, offer Godly counsel and pray at the end of our conversation. I was able to call her at anytime, which I did not abuse by calling too late because I respected her time and marriage. I was able to tell her anything and it stayed in the confinement of her home. We developed a Mother and Daughter relationship and I am eternally grateful for the impact she had on my life. God bless her soul; she has gone on to be with the Lord in 2018. If I had allowed her appearance at the time to stop me from getting to know her I would have missed a God ordained opportunity that took me from where I was to where God wanted me to be.

Your Drive in Life

Some people were born into families where they were well cared for, encouraged and supported, while others did not have this luxury. I remember when growing up, there were people in the community who would buy my siblings and myself school clothes and some people would have given us food to eat, because my parents were not sufficiently financially stable to provide for the eight of us along with paying bills, and buying food. However, they did the little they could with the little they had. I remembered not doing well in the Eleven Plus Examination, which is an exam we took in order to be placed in Secondary School, because of not having the required textbooks and the support needed to do my homework and schoolwork in preparation for the exam.

I felt at that moment like I had let many people down who thought I would have done better. I was able to go to what was called the lowest secondary school because of my marks. I was not a Christian at the time, but I remember that I knelt down and prayed to God to help me to be able to read and get through secondary school because I wanted to leave School with Caribbean Examination Council (CXC) certifications at the end of my journey at school. God granted me my heart's desires; he taught me how to read and write. I was always at the top of my class and I became the Head Girl. On leaving school, I obtained seven CXCs. God is a faithful God and he hears our every prayer; if we believe, he will move mountains to accomplish in our lives what seems impossible and futile. I went on to the Barbados Community College and then the University of the West Indies, and later in life I did my master's with the University of Liverpool. Do not try to convince me that God is dead; he is surely alive today and forevermore. He reminds us in the bible that he is the good Shepherd and if he is the good Shepherd he will supply everyone of your needs and give you an expected end. I lacked nothing, I was able to accomplish like those who were born in fortunate families and I felt like I had the same privileges as they did.

I would say I was well taken care of by God and the people he had placed in my life at each juncture. It was as if each person came at the right time to pass on the baton to the next helper; for this reason I felt like nothing was missing. Even though I had to work to send myself to school at the latter part of my tenure at secondary school, I know it was God who provided the jobs I needed to get the money I used to go to school. Yes, it was difficult but I always had the drive in me to succeed so I would always think ahead, set targets and go after my dreams. This drive, even though it was good, created divisions among my siblings, as they would always think that I thought I was better than them or I thought I was more important than them. I would always try to encourage them to do better and would always help financially because I wanted them to achieve as well.

I always felt like the odd one out, as though I did not belong. I often asked myself, "Why am I so different from my siblings and why do I feel like I am not needed?" Rejection from the ones closest to you, such as your blood family, can have many negative impacts on your self-image, worth, joy and happiness. It was like *'pulling teeth'* even to have a basic

49

conversation, because the way we saw the world and life was different. This caused me to have those kinds of conversations with people who were on the same mental and intellectual level but I still longed for the sibling to sibling conversations.

Your Family Tree

Some might think that we just appeared here on planet earth without taking into consideration their ancestral connection. Everyone has a mother, a grand-mother, a great-grand-mother and it goes as far back as to Adam and Eve in the Garden of Eden. Each family has something that identifies them with their family through the generations, whether it is something good or bad. I know of a family, because of generational curses (which are negative occurrences which have been passed on from the previous generation to the next one), where the father was in jail and all of his sons ended up in jail as well. God promises us "life and that ... more abundantly" (John 10:10, KJV), not to be locked away behind bars not fulfilling our purpose or making a positive difference in the lives of those around us. I know it is difficult to break these chain links but the power of God is able to break every chain that has been set up to keep you in bondage. The bible is clear when it says in Luke 4:18 (NLT) that, "The Spirit of the Lord is upon me, for he has anointed me to bring Good News to the poor. He has sent me to proclaim that captives will be released, that the blind will see, that the oppressed will be set free..."

I believe that some people have an innate drive to succeed and some people find it difficult to make a start. This can be a factor in many things, including the type of environment they were raised in, because some environments can be criticising, speaking failure into your life, which can cause you to be de-motivated. If you are not a self-motivated person, not having the support and encouragement needed can cause stagnation. *The Spirit of the Lord is upon me, for he has anointed me to bring Good News to the poor. He has sent me to proclaim that captives will be released, that the blind will see, that the oppressed will be set free*".

If we took the time to trace our family lineage, we would discover a lot of things about our family and about ourselves that we would not have been able to shed light on. I remember in my early teens, being a young Christian, not fully understanding what connection any of my ancestors had with me. Sometimes bad things will continue to reoccur in our lives and our children's lives until we are made aware, are willing to confront, and are willing to confess and turn from them. In my family, I identified the trends of poverty, laziness, procrastination, disunity and unforgiveness. I was the first person in my family to have gotten a University degree and my youngest sister followed a few years after. I was the first to have gotten a decent job working in a commercial bank, which was only mainly attained by families in the heights and terraces. Many people in my community looked up to me as a young progressive lady; some of whom I was not aware until I moved out of my parents' house in my early thirties. We never know whose lives we are impacting by the way we carry ourselves and in how we push against the odds to achieve our goals – through Christ, of course. We can do all things through him, once we put our confidence and faith in him and follow his precepts. In the old Testament, God is called the God of Abraham, Isaac and Jacob, why was this? He has made a covenant of promise and purpose with their forefathers, and all of their descendants. We see here that a blessing or a curse can follow from generation to generation. There are also certain traits and characteristics, known by present generations, which could be found in their looks, personality, way of life ,that can be traced back to the third generation of the family, or in some cases before. For instance, a family who has males who are 6 feet tall, dark, have brown eyes and who talk with a dramatic voice are known by that family for generations. The diagram below shows the trace from you to as far back as many generations where a blessing or a curse was identified.

Trace of Family Tree

Once you have identified the blessing, praise God; on the other hand, once you have identified the curse, what is the next step? The first step will be to ask God for his forgiveness, even though it was not you who committed the crime. It might not be you, but because the transgressor is connected to you through your lineage, it will continue to have a legal right to manifest and do its ugly work in your life and in the life of your family. This is done through confession of the wrong or wrongs and asking God for his forgiveness. The next step will be to turn from the sins that grieve God. This means to stop committing the wrongful acts; then God will forgive and heal your land. The next step after that is to accept and enjoy his forgiveness, walk in it and receive the blessings which God has promised to the children of obedience. This does not mean that bad things will not happen in your life, but you will be more easily able to identify the blessings and curses. Also, praying always for your family that they too will turn from their wicked ways and come under the blessings of God. This process will save many recurrences of negative cycles, which were hiding in the trace of the family tree through its many generations of *the same old, same old thing* – some of which are easy to identify and some will take some time to research and realize; either way it is worth the effort. Here is a simple prayer that can save you and your family from reaping the same curses over and over and over again.

"Dear God, I come to you in the name of our Lord and Saviour Jesus Christ, I repent of the sins of my fore-parents, my parents and myself. I acknowledge that we have sinned against you and I ask for your forgiveness. Wash us in your blood and set us free from every sin, bondage and evil cycle in Jesus name. Amen."
Thank Him for the marvellous work he has started in your life and He is able to keep you until his return. Walk in the freedom which God has intended for you to walk in and your children and their children's children. Chapter Four looks closely at the effects rejection can have on a person who experiences it.

CHAPTER FIVE:
Effects of Rejection

Who likes to be rejected? No one. Rejection can have many effects on a person, which can cause them to withdraw from wanting to be around other people. Moreover, it can have negative effects on one's mind, self-image, self-esteem and emotions. Some of these effects can last a lifetime if not dealt with as they surface. This chapter seeks to explain some of the effects that rejection can have on a person.

Psychological

Rejection in itself is a negative experience which can have effects on our minds, which are connected to our emotions. A person's perception of self and others is coined in the thoughts and beliefs they have about themselves. This shapes the way we see our realities and the world around us. I can remember comments made by my family when I was young that today still linger in my mind, which affect how

I view myself and how I relate to other people. People would ask, "Are you a boy or a girl?"

I actually started to believe this; I told myself that I like outdoor activities and I developed breasts late – that made it more convincing to me. I thought I was not good looking and, at one point, I started to be attracted to the same sex, but never pursued any relationships in that way because of my Church background. I knew it was wrong, but it was how I felt. It took years for me to believe that I was beautiful. Guess what? God caused people to actually call me beautiful and I knew God was using these people to reassure me that I was, indeed, beautiful. I began to speak it, to look in the mirror and tell myself, "I am beautiful". As I did that, it came forth brighter and brighter until I saw it and believed it. The words still echo in the back of my mind but positive reinforcement wins. Your experience might be different from mine but if we believe these thoughts, they become our reality. This calls for positive reinforcement; when the negative thoughts appear, speak the positive. Don't for one second agree with what the enemy is saying to you. God has a perfect plan for your life and he has the best in store for you. Thoughts like, "I am not beautiful", "I will never be happy", and "Life is not worth living." Rather speak words of optimism, like "I am fearfully and wonderfully made," Psalm 139:14 (KJV); "The joy of the Lord is my strength", Psalm 28:7 (KJV); and "The Spirit of God has made me, and the breath of the Almighty hath given me life." Job 33:4 (KJV). Our mind is like a computer; what we have put into it ourselves or by others is stored there until the opportune time to show up on our monitor, which in this case is our mind. It is a process that can take some time, but the most important thing is to make the start or get the help needed to overcome this hurdle that can keep you in bondage for a very long time.

Depression

God has provided everything for us to live an enjoyable, healthy and happy life. This is possible through our redemption, his word and the anointing that breaks every yoke. On the contrary, if depression is happening in your life, I want to let you know that it is not of God. According to Colossians 1:27, he is our hope in glory. If God is a spirit and he brings joy then depression is also a spirit that brings despair. The one you yield your mind to is the one that will conquer you. When the stronghold of rejection stays in your life, depression settles in. It then becomes a part of who you are: your personality is one of pessimism; you are always finding the most negative things to say in every situation instead of seeing the positive side to your circumstances. Then you begin to accept these lies and you can begin to speak them into existence. That forms the stronghold in your mind and in your life that has to be broken before freedom can come. We are created in the image of God. Because of this, the same way he spoke and the world was created, we too can speak and it creates our world around us. See Proverbs 18:21 (KJV), which says "Death and life are in the power of the tongue: And they that love it shall eat the fruit thereof".

In my early twenties, having gone through so many traumatic experiences, I was very depressed to the point of suicide. I could see no hope and I thought that was the best thing to do. The enemy would tell me, "God does not love you. Drive your car at top speed on the highway and kill yourself." I knew if I did that I would end up in hell right where the devil wanted me to be. I had to believe that God has a plan for my life, he loves me and that things will get better. Depression is so powerful that if we allow it to dominate our lives, it can take the very life that Jesus has suffered, bled and died for us to have. Having no one to talk to or keeping everything buckled up inside makes it worse. It is very important during this time to find a Pastor, a Church Leader, a Counsellor or a trusted mature adult, family relative or friend in whom you can confide. Imagine a river with one side blocked up. What do you think will happen to the debris in the river? It will become contaminated, rot and begin to smell. It is the same thing that happens when we keep all the past baggage and negative emotions inside – it begins to pollute our lives and gives off a bad odour when we encounter people from day to day. These emotions are seen in the way we behave; felt by the presence we carry and can manifest in many ailments and sicknesses in or bodies

At one point, just being around people triggered feelings of sadness. I avoided crowds or people as much as possible, which was how low and depressed I was. Being sad and depressed is like death, it kills your desire for life and happiness and your acceptance of love from others. It is a mindset and belief of a situation we have experienced or are going through. I have a hard time hiding my emotions, so it actually shows on my face. Some people who are depressed tend to have their head down all the time, they wear a frown on their face and the tone of their voice is usually sad. Unconsciously, people with this condition, most of the time, are drawn to places that have few people around, or none at all. Depression can take away your energy, to the point where you become lazy, and procrastination is the catch of the day. If you are in a state of helplessness, with feelings of sadness, for a consistently long period of time, there is always help before it gets worse. Some people may find that the things they once enjoyed are not pleasurable anymore and that they have no interest in them. The situations that made us low in spirit are the centre of our attention. Going to bed and waking up do not have the joy and meaningfulness as they once did and eating can be unappetising as it now becomes something we don't feel like doing.

Suicidal Thoughts

The enemy knows when to launch his attacks on our minds – when we are at our lowest. This is the opportune time, where he comes with his lies whispering in our ears that it does not make any sense going on. "You will be better off not being here and no one will miss you. Just end it now and put an end to your pain and misery." The more we allow these thoughts to live in our minds, the more power is given to the enemy to have his way with our lives.

The mind has the ability to convince our emotions that what we are thinking is our reality. Then it is fed to our actions, which causes us to put our thoughts into action. This is how the power is transferred and we are defeated. The bible is the greatest book that has been ever written, and it gives us a word when we really need it – just one word to lift us out of the mental bondage we can find ourselves under. When God created man, he breathed life into his nostrils and he became a living soul. Why then should we try to take what was given to us as a gift from our heavenly Father? God is the one who will take our breath when he is ready to promote us to glory. This means that anything that wants to take it is a thief. The enemy comes to kill, steal and destroy but God came to give life and to give it more abundantly. (John 10:10)

What we spend the most of our time focusing on eventually becomes our reality. Philippians 4:8 (KJV) reminds us that *"Finally, brethren, whatsoever things are true, whatsoever things are honest, whatsoever things are just, whatsoever things are pure, whatsoever things are lovely, whatsoever things are of good report; if there be any virtue, and if there be any praise, think on these things."* The easiest thing to do is to worry, and to think of the worst case scenario in a situation that seems hopeless, instead of declaring and decreeing what the bible says until it becomes our reality.

Thinking positive thoughts in spite of what you are faced with gives you strength instantly and it puts you on the rebound from what seemed so impossible. God sees our true love for him when we profess his words over our lives and situations. This invites his presence to come and do what only he can do, breaking every negative chain of despair, which wants us to take the very life he has given us to enjoy and to be a blessing to the persons we encounter along our journey.

Anger, Anxiety & Aggression

The three A's, Anger, Anxiety and Aggression, when broken down, can be a deadly pill if ingested. Everyone wants to be accepted by someone or some group; it is in our DNA, we need each other. Imagine living in a world with people but not interacting with them and this becomes a norm for you.

What do you think will happen? You become a prisoner in your mind to the people around you and sadness becomes your best friend. Rejection added to this makes it a perfect recipe for anger to thrive. Because these emotions are bottled up inside, they eventually will cause you to outwardly express them in a harmful way, which can cause emotional or, in some cases physical, pain to self or others. Let's take a look at each element to understand its linkages to the captivity in our lives.

Anger – A strong negative emotion which is oftentimes triggered by unfortunate circumstances. Anger is a feeling which, like all feelings, means that it can be altered to birth feelings of joy and happiness in its place. It is easy to dwell on negative thoughts when all around us seems dim and the atmosphere over our lives feels heavy, it is more convincing to agree with feelings that are destructive to our lives.

Anxiety – An emotion which is classified as feelings of tension and, in some cases, having worrisome thoughts which can alter changes in one's blood pressure. It is known as a disorder which causes continuous thoughts to consume a person and brings on some level of uneasiness. If you are a victim of this condition, remember that God has promised you a sound mind. It is easy to worry and get all worked up about situations that oftentimes are not as bad as we may think. This steals your joy and peace of mind, which can stop you from living a fulfilling and happy life.

Aggression – A verbal or physical behaviour which can be threatening to another person or self. In some cases it can be diverted to objects, animals or what is used by the person at the time to cause harm to him or herself or the target. This destructive behaviour can cause you to lose family, friends or partners because of the negative effects it can

have on them emotionally, physically or psycholo-
gically.

CHAPTER SIX:
The Pain of Rejection

This chapter seeks to explain the **emotions** which are triggered by the pain caused by rejection. Who likes rejection? No hands will be raised for this question, because everyone will try their best to avoid bad experiences and cling to the good experiences that bring joy and happiness. The thought of being isolated or picked on and being on the list of the least liked is not a good place to be in, especially when you have done nothing to deserve it. This oftentimes scares our feelings and can result in depression and sadness.

. Imagine the life that Jesus lived, forsaking everyone and staying on his path to rescue us from eternal damnation. This was not an easy task to have done, walking a lonesome road when the only one he could have totally relied on and who did not forsake him was the Father. When Jesus really wanted his disciples to have been there for him at his critical time of need they were asleep. The good thing about this is that Jesus knows the pain you're going through because he was there, a long time ago but even though time has changed his love and relevance to your unique situation is a great opportunity for him to show up and show off his sovereignty in your life.

As we have read in previous chapters, that rejection can leave many scars and, in some cases, ones that last up to a lifetime. When rejection comes knocking at our door, it brings with it unworthiness as a companion. People will look down on others and overlook their value once they have rejected them and have seen them as worthless; their true worth and value is then hidden, which can make them feel unloved. This can lead to self-hatred, where the rejection is turned inward and the victim begins to hate themselves because no one seems to see who they really are and accept them as part of their lives. Feelings of envy can creep in because the victim begins to compare themselves to other people and wish that they had looked, talked, acted like others, or even wish they had what others had. They begin to tell themselves, "If I had these traits, qualities or possessions, I would be accepted by others."

It is the enemy's plan to make us feel unloved and unaccepted by others. God is saying, "I love you, my child, and envy is not of me, I have good plans in store for you and I will reveal them in my time." We were not created to allow these emotions to control us, but rather to allow the Holy Spirit to have power over our emotional well-being.

Once a negative emotion is planted in our heart, it begins to grow, mature and bear fruit. The **H.T.A.** Emotional Cycle has three components. These are highlighted as the **Heart**, the **Thoughts** and the **Actions**. Our **heart** is the soil. Every time we experience rejection, it sows emotional seeds into the soil of our heart. Our **thoughts** are the manure; once the emotional seeds are planted, they are then fed by what we think of ourselves and the situation, which it finally produces fruits in accordance with our **actions**. This cycle will continue to repeat itself until we decide to make some changes in each stage of the H.T.A. Emotional Cycle. The keys are all in our hands. With God's help and divine intervention, every power that is causing us to repeat this dreaded cycle, we command it to break right now in Jesus mighty name. Amen.

Embrace the fruits of the spirit as highlighted in Galatians 5:22-23 (NIV):

"22 But the fruit of the Spirit is love, joy, peace, forbearance, kindness, goodness,faithfulness, 23 gentleness and self-control. Against such things there is no law."

Jesus intends for us to live a fruitful life as we journey through this earth. As a believer in Jesus Christ, our lives should bring forth fruits of the spirit that surpass what emotional state we might be experiencing. The first two fruits of the spirit are love and joy, which are the keys needed to unlock our hearts to release the garbage that has been planted by the enemy, others and in some cases ourselves. These fruits are like the medicine needed to cure a heart that has been broken.

Our thoughts are so powerful, that they feed the soil of our heart with the nutrients it needs to produce a plant that is either healthy or unhealthy . As we get rid of the weak contaminated manure, we begin to feed our thoughts the word of God, which dispels the darkness and causes our lives to be healthy and meaningful.

Our actions did not just occur, there is a process which we would have gone through, knowingly or unknowingly, to arrive at the actions which are being seen. For instance, someone committing a premeditated murder usually did not just wake up from sleeping one morning and kill someone. He conceived it in his heart, and then the right manure, which are the thoughts of anger, hatred, and revenge, caused him to carry out the act of murder. The thoughts cycled until they produced the desired action.

Unworthiness

When we internalise rejection, we begin to see ourselves as unworthy. It can become a condition of how you view yourself and how people perceive you. This can cause you to look for areas of your life that you think are not acceptable and blame these areas to justify your reasons for feeling unworthy. You may think that you are not intelligent enough, pretty, or attractive enough. This is what the enemy of our souls wants us to believe, so that we can lower our standards and live a defeated life. The good news is that Jesus took the chastisement for us, so why do we punish ourselves for what has already been paid for by our loving Heavenly Father? God accepts us just the way we are, why then do we try to make perfect what is imperfect, only the Creator has that ability. So we have some work to do on how we view ourselves and our imperfections. We are fearfully and wonderfully made by a perfect God who took the time out to carve our bodies in his image and gave us many unique features that we can feel proud of having. What you may hate about yourself someone appreciates and wishes they had, so be grateful for what God has done. I remember, in my teenage years, I thought I had unattractive eyes, which made me always look away when having a conversation. However, today I thank God for my pretty brown eyes. If the King of Kings accepts you, you are worth more than a priceless possession. Amen.

Self Hatred

Hate is a very strong emotion, which is birthed out of an offence, how you view yourself and the experiences in life that were not favourable to you. If God does not hate us why do we hate ourselves? This again is a plan of the enemy of our souls, to cause us to point all fingers inward, locking ourselves in from accepting where we are, how we are and releasing ourselves from our own prison. This prison, most of the time, is located in our minds: being prideful, not wanting to let anyone in your space and spiritual cages. This is where we need a Pastor or Deliverance Minister to take us through the process of setting us free from oppression, depression, anger, hatred, unforgiveness and from how we perceive things in our minds. For God so loved the world that he gave. What did he give? His only begotten son. Why? So that we may have life and have it in abundance. What is stopping you? Sometimes the level of hate we have for ourselves robs us of receiving the life Christ has sacrificed for us to have because we think we don't deserve his love and forgiveness. When we begin to love ourselves it starts the process of reconciliation, joy, happiness and forgiveness, which our Father wants for us more than we want for ourselves. Always remember that hatred is not of God, so you don't need it. The ball is in your court; the longer it is there the longer your situation will remain the same. The first thing is to accept that you have a problem; I know this is the hardest thing to do, especially when the issue is with ourselves. This process may cause pain and crying but the end result is worth the effort.

The second thing is to start moving, get the help you need to move from where you are to where God wants you to be, which is to be free. The next thing is to follow through with the necessary steps that will take you from self hatred to self love. The keys are all in your hand, waiting for you to open the door that leads to freedom.

Envy

Rejection, whether intentional or unintentional, as we are aware, can have detrimental effects on us, even if we may consider ourselves as strong people. The role of parents is very important in nurturing and affirming your children that they are fearfully and wonderfully made by God. This assurance can save them from accepting others' definition of them and more importantly accepting what God says about them. He says in Psalm 139:14 that we are fearfully and wonderfully made. God has given us everything we need to live a life of happiness and fulfilment and there will be no need for being envious. This is a strategy of the devil to cause you to look at others and want what they have that you lack and then you begin to develop feelings of envy. The bible warns us that we should not be ignorant of the enemy's devices. His operations are very intelligent and he was around longer than anyone of us. God has already provided everything we need in this life for he knew us even before we were formed in our Mother's womb. Search your house! What do you have in it? They are treasures no man has seen or even heard of waiting for the right time and season to evolve to the front of your life. Live, laugh and enjoy each moment along the way.

Rejection, if not dealt with, can have many negative implications on all aspects of our lives. Some people, because of the continuous experience of rejection, can become **aggressive**, which is a violent behaviour that can destroy many good relationships. Most people would rather not be around someone who is always hostile or ill-mannered. This can lead to self hurt in some cases and the hurt of others. If we are in Christ, then we ought to engage the bowels of compassion, knowing that we are accepted in the beloved. This aggressive behaviour in the end – guess what? It hurts you the most; it is displacing your inner turmoil on to someone who does not deserve it. Imagine the gym trainer seeing you struggling during a session and adding an extra 10 pounds when you are exhausted by the weights you are already using. Although his intentions could have been to push you beyond your comfort zone, you might interpret his actions as him wanting to harm you physically by seeing you struggling and increasing the pain, making it a challenge for you. It can make you want to react in a negative manner, but situations present themselves to test our ability to demonstrate self-control, which is part of the fruit of the spirit.

Physical Pain

The **physical pain** we experience in our bodies can sometimes be caused by the emotions triggered by rejection. Once it is not released and the person(s) who have rejected us are not forgiven, it can create many health challenges. Researchers have proven this point to be true by the amount of people who develop all types of cancers because of negative emotions such as unforgiveness, which creates the fertile ground for acidity, the home for cancer to thrive. The pain of being rejected can cause people to develop eating disorders, for some they can eat throughout the day, as the pain comes, food is their comfort, their way to escape. On the other hand, some people may eat less or not at all for long periods of time, developing, in some cases, stomach disorders, malnutrition, loss of weight, loss of appetite and anorexia. Some people may experience pain in their chest; this can be a result of the negative emotions built up over time and not released. Abnormal sleeping patterns such as insomnia may also develop, not being able to experience the sweet sleep God promises us in the Bible.

Proverbs 3:24 (KJV) "When thou liest down, thou shalt not be afraid: yea, thou shalt lie down, and thy sleep shall be sweet".

Spiritual Pain

A crushed soul can rob us of truly experiencing all that God has created for us to have and enjoy. Life is seen as meaningless and this oftentimes leads to depression and isolation. Imagine trying to cheer up someone who is broken; it will be a difficult task to accomplish. Our soul, which encapsulates our mind, emotions and intellect, drives our everyday actions and is responsible for the reasons behind those actions, which are rooted in our experiences and how we view the world around us. Yes, the memories of past pain and hurts will always be there, but it is the approach and strategies we adopt to overcome these hurdles that allow us to live in the now and not as a captive of our past. When our spirit is broken, it affects our entire being, as we first are spirit then body. In situations of pain we tend to lean to our own understanding, forsaking running to Jesus who is there willing and able to lift us up by his love. In some cases we wallow in self-pity, not wanting to read the bible, pray or spend time in the presence of God or even with our Church family. This is a very dangerous place to be, especially if you don't have the support and spiritual covering to ward off the attacks that want to come and oppress you.

The battle starts in the mind and once this is conquered by the enemy he has won. Without the head we have no sense of direction or control over where we are going and it will prevent us from making sound decisions. Always remember to have a journal handy to make notes everyday of how you truly feel and next to them write what God says which is his *rhema* word, then decree and declare it over your life until you see the manifestation evident in your life. The words we speak have power to create our realities: in other words, you are what you think. For every negative thought, replace it with two or more positive thoughts. Spend time in the word of God; this is where he speaks to us and shows us his salvation in the darkest moments in life. As you practice this it becomes a daily routine that will transform your life. Another way of over-coming spiritual pain is by spending quality time in the presence of God. It is in the times of brokenness he re-energies us by his sweet Holy Spirit, for in the presence of the Lord there is fullness of joy where pain decreases and joy increases.

There is a saying, which I find to be so insightful: *"Hurt people hurt people."* Reflecting on this, it speaks of a truth that if you are hurting the only thing you know best is to hurt others. It has become a part of your DNA which reproduces pain and hurt. Imagine stumping an injured toe over and over be-fore it is restored to health. If this pain is not healed completely, it can cause some of the people divinely sent by God to help you to have a very difficult time or to just leave you in the state they found you in because of the level of work it would take to bring you to a place of freedom. The next chapter will seek to explain the ultimate outcome that can result after the process of rejection is complete, for there is always a reason beyond our understanding. It also promises to take a close look at the purpose of rejection. Oftentimes, this is overlooked, and the main reason for the rejection is not realised.

CHAPTER SEVEN:
The Purpose of Rejection

Who would imagine a purpose coming out of rejection? All we can see when experiencing rejection is what is negative, unfortunate and gloomy. The 'now' is as far as we can see, as we wallow in self pity and sorrow. This tends to temporarily numb the pain you are going through as a way to cover the scars. To illustrate this point, consider peeling an onion. You would realize that it has rings going around in a circle, a ring on top of a ring, from the top to the bottom.

This can be related to the scar of each bad experience encircling you, with you seemingly unable to break free from it, and with each corresponding bad experience piling another 'circle' on top of the first one. This cycle would continue until the circles are identified and dealt with. In some scenarios it can be easier for some people than others to triumph over these overwhelming situations, as all of us are created uniquely by the Creator. This means that our coping mechanisms are vast and can be pinned to our childhood experiences, which follow us into adulthood and our beliefs and perceptions about the world are the pillars on which we tend to build our defences. The magnitude of our bad experiences makes it easier to form more and more rings, which makes it difficult to break. We tend to do what makes it easy to sweep the pain under the carpet in hopes that no one realises that it is there. We don't want to acknowledge, or be honest with ourselves, that there is an issue. The first step towards freedom, however, is acknowledging that there is a problem, then confronting the issue, then getting the requisite help in order to be able to walk in that freedom. Is it easy? No, but as you take the first step the process will begin. It might take weeks, months and in some cases years, depending on the level of hurt and pain you have experienced, but you are assured that it will be worth the effort, so *'no more delay'*. Set a date in your diary and start the journey, God promises you complete freedom and healing as you walk through the P R O C E S S.

Each and everyone one on planet earth was born for a purpose and with a purpose given by God himself. Some people find it early in their life and some later in life and some whom might need help in identifying it, but it is there once we take the time to look for it and identify it. Jeremiah 29: 11 (KJV), reiterates the point that God has a plan for our lives and he will work his will out in spite of how you may be feeling, to give you hope and a bright future. God's thoughts towards us are good thoughts and he wants us to prosper in every aspect of our lives. Sometimes it is the simple yet profound things in life we may just need, it might be just to know someone cares, just to have a friend or someone close to listen to us, in an objective way, or a simple hug, which goes a very long way for the recipient.

How Do You Find Your Purpose?

Let's start by identifying what 'purpose' is. We know that it is God breathed, it involves the reason why we exist to begin with. When God created Adam in the book of Genesis 2:15, he had a purpose for him to work the Garden of Eden and to take care of it. Imagine being in a beautiful garden and enjoying it, not to mention listening to the birds chirping and seeing the flowers blooming, having permission to eat from the fruit trees God commanded us to eat from, and – most importantly – to have communion with him. One word to describe this scene is simply AWESOME. God did not only put Adam in the Garden of Eden, but he created the right environment for him to thrive in by setting the tone for a peaceful and tranquil life as he traversed the Garden. I love nature especially hiking, it is very therapeutic and it allows me to enjoy and appreciate God's creation, which brings fulfilment and relaxation. He knew Adam would need someone to help him and to accompany him in the Garden, so guess what? He created a helpmate, Eve, in Genesis 2: 21-22 (KJV) from Adam's rib, and instructed them to be fruitful and multiply.

Sometimes we look for the 'highfalutin' things in life and they are simple, just being here on earth and being alive is purpose in itself. We never know the magnitude of our presence in the lives of others by just simply being a part of them. It makes a great difference by adding value to their lives and sometimes they might not realize it until you are not in their life for whatever the reason may be. Some of the possible reasons for this could be that the friendship has ended naturally, you moved to another country, you both grew apart, or you died, among many other scenarios encountered in life.

We always tend to gravitate towards what we have a passion for and what we love. I remember on evenings after school, while being on the long bus ride home in the countryside from the bus terminal, I would take out my book and pen and start to write little poems, which I later read at Church. It is something I love to do, to sit quietly and just start to write. For me it comes easily, writing about God's love and current emotions I was feeling or current societal situations that I believed needed my input. Later in life I realised that songs were just an extension of poetry so I began writing songs; the only thing I needed was voice training. It is my intention to sing some of the songs I have written to inspire others.

Everyone is born with a talent or multiple talents, for some it might be just being hospitable, sharing a kind word, helping in charitable organizations, writing, singing, dancing, preaching, Pastoring, being a good businessman, planning, advising and the list goes on. They are also **natural gifts** and **spiritual gifts** as I would categorise them. The natural ones are the ones we use to enhance our physical livelihood, for instance being the best shoemaker or dressmaker in town that everyone goes to when they need help with shoes and clothing. On the other hand, 1 Corinthians 12: 7 highlights the gifts of the Holy Spirit, which are given for the edification of the Church. No matter how insignificant you might think your gift is, someone somewhere is waiting to be blessed by it. From this, we can see that our gifts are not only for us to enjoy but they are people who are connected to those giftings who God will send your way or cause you to be connected to them for the purpose of sharing what you have with them. After all, why send them elsewhere for the same blessing when you have it in your hands? Now we can see the bigger picture that our purpose is connected to so many people we are not even aware of as yet.

Everything you have been through in life is the preparation stage for something bigger, stay tuned as God begins to mould you and shape you through the painful process. Nothing worthwhile just appears, it has to go through a process of refinement in order to be of any value when it is done. Endure, stay in the fight, don't look to the left nor to the right, keep your eyes fixed on Jesus and he will take you to your destiny in a limousine. Take a look at Esther – before she became queen she had to go through a process of purification to be able to wear the royal apparel and play her part well. Imagine coming from an orphan girl to the queen, people only see the glorious transformation but the hard work behind the curtains, away from the public's vantage point, is oftentimes missed. For the full story, please see Esther chapter 2. The same way God prepared Esther is the same way he will prepare you for the purpose he has created you for, as you yield and surrender your will to his will for your life.

Once you find your purpose in life it brings joy, peace and fulfilment. It can be compared to when a woman is pregnant and has to go through the different trimester stages and then she finally experiences the birth pains before bringing forth her lovely bundle of joy. When this happens she forgets all the pain she had to go through but, rather, focuses on her beautiful baby in front of her. Being able to help others after the pain and hurt of rejections is worth the process, to see the joy on people's faces you are able to encourage them along their walk in life. Always remember that nothing in life just happens, as God has created us with a purpose to fulfil.

Jesus knew his purpose early in life at the tender age of twelve in Luke 9, (NKJV). It says, *"And He said to them, 'Why did you seek Me? Did you not know that I must be about My Father's business?'"*. He was already focused, from a very young age, on fulfilling his purpose here on earth and he was determined that no one distracted him from doing so. Living a purposeful life brings a zeal and passion to achieve your vision. You might say that at a young age you should not be taking life so seriously but success comes with commitment and sacrifice, giving up the things we love to achieve greatness. I am sure he played but he did not let it pull him away from his purpose, as time is of the essence, it waits on no man. It paid off – thank you Jesus – that at the age of 33 ½ he completed his purpose on earth and now we can be redeemed. If we ask him for the forgiveness of our sins, we will live with him forever, Hallelujah! Glory to his name most high! Once you find your purpose do not let procrastination win over you, but write the vision down, make it plain and run with it until you reach the finish line. I am sure you want to hear, "Well done, thou good and faithful servant." (Matthew 25:21) After all, we are here to serve God and serve each other through purpose.

Chapter Eight: The Joy of Rejection

This chapter seeks to bring to life the realisation that there can be joy in the midst of rejection. A typical example can be found in Genesis Chapter 37:27-36 (KJV), where Joseph's brothers disliked him, rejected him and sold him to Potiphar the Captain of Pharaoh's guard, into slavery in Egypt, but little did they know that it was the preparation stage he had to go through before he became Chief Overseer of the food. The act of throwing him in a pit , then selling him to some passing merchants, was done by the ones who came from the same father , the same household, and who shared the same biological makeup; this brings to reality the fact that everyone in the same household or from the same family might not be on your team as much as you might be on theirs.

Everything you have been through has prepared you for where God is taking you, buckle up and get ready for the ride that leads to *joyland*. Let's look a little closer at the life of Joseph and his journey to becoming a leader in the land he was sold into. He was the brother of eleven siblings and his father Jacob favoured him more than his other brothers. This created a hatred for Joseph, even though he was oblivious to the way they felt about him. To add fuel to the fire, he had the gift of the interpretation of dreams and because of this, he was elated to have shared his dream with his brothers, which included them bowing down before him, but this made them hate him even more, as they thought he was being arrogant. All they wanted to do was to get rid of him. They wanted this so badly that they were looking for the first best opportunity to do so.

Looking at this story with a magnifying glass, you will realize that everything was orchestrated by God for him to be taken to Egypt. The merchants who passed the particular day he was sold were not going to another country, they were going to Egypt for a reason. Everything that you have been through was just the preparation stage for purpose to spring forth. Through the process it brings maturity, knowledge, understanding and the strengthening of the skills we need to fill the position God has ordained for us to fulfil.

God caused the prisoner whom Joseph assisted by interpreting his dream to have remembered him at a time Pharaoh needed an interpreter. This opportunity landed him right where God wanted him to be in order for his dream and purpose to be fulfilled. It might take years, but guess what? It will come to pass as you stay the course and allow God to order your steps each step of the way. In the end Joseph counted it all joy because he saw the good in everything he had been through and to have lived to see his dream come to pass, while being of service to the people of Egypt and abroad in a time of famine and great need. The story could have taken a negative spin, but it did not, because it was to give us the example that we should not focus on the wrong people have done unto us but to see purpose in it and how we can use it to bless others in their time of need. Remember, it is not about us! Rather see it as a non-negotiable process you had to go through in order to develop you to become the leader and destiny fulfiller he has on his books for you. Leaders don't just evolve; they have to face the pain, hurt, tears and sorrow to become all they were born to become. I am sure Joseph was not superhuman, he felt the pain of rejection and hurt, which stirred up emotions that made him cry. An athlete, I am sure, can agree that in order to win, you have to go through rigorous training, follow a strict diet plan and give up many pleasurable things in order to compete against the world's finest athletes. This process puts them in a competitive shape and position for the race of their life when the day has come. Most importantly, when you win the race, the pain is put aside and the joy of achieving your goal of winning the race brings fulfilment and momentum to push yourself to achieve greater the next time around.

It is easy to see and focus on the now and everything you are going through, in your wilderness experience. This clouds your vision of what God could be up to in your life. Funny enough, many of us ask God to make us – for instance – a powerful preacher, but when the process begins we begin to say, "Ouch, Lord I can't make it, take it away!" If you ask God for it, be willing to go through the obstacle course and come out victorious. He will not leave you; he is your helper and he will Shepherd you along the journey. If he knew you were not capable, he would not have given you the critical part to play in his beautiful picture. You are important, your part will not play without you, it is needed to have the full effects and meaning of the beautiful art work. .

Below is a short quiz on what is referred to as the 'Joseph's experience' in your life and how it impacted you. If you are still going through your process, you can still participate as far as possible. Fill in the blanks as God begins to break every stronghold still wanting to keep you captive from fully walking out your experience and may the peace of God rule and reign in your life today and forevermore. Amen.

Joseph's Experience:

Event..

Year................

Describe what happened?...

....

....

....

....

....

....

....

How did you feel through the process?................................

....

....

....

What kept you through the process?................................

....

....

....

What one thing do you believe God used you to accomplish?

....

....

....

How do you feel now having gone through the experience?....

....

....

What is your takeaway?..

....

....

....

Prayer: Our heavenly Father, we come to you in the name of your Son Jesus Christ. We pray God that you will heal the hearts of those who have experienced rejection, pain and hurt. I pray that you will heal them and that they will receive your comfort and strength to go through the process and receive healing and fulfilment and ultimately, may they receive the joy this experience brings to them. These things we ask in Jesus' name with thanksgiving. Amen.

CHAPTER NINE:
Final Thoughts

Rejection, pain and negative emotions are a part of life; they come at some point in our lives to teach us a lesson, and to help us to grow into the persons God has ordained us to be. If you have or might be experiencing rejection, go through the process; remember, it is not about you but about those whom God will send your way to receive what has been deposited into your life. It is only at the end of the tunnel that you will see the reasons for it. God said he will never give us more than we can bear. When it is all over you will be wiser, stronger and in a better position to help someone who might be faced with a similar situation.

Rejection is never easy to deal with because all of us were created to feel accepted and to have a sense of worth. Our response to rejection determines how long we stay in the same place before we can graduate from the place of abandonment to a place of acceptance, peace, happiness and fulfilment. God is still able to make wine from water, what seems impossible with man is possible with him; he is able to add value to your life and to make it a priceless blessing. For the race is not for the swift but for the ones who will ensure the journey until the very end. You don't have to walk alone, for they are more for you than those who are against you. The Father, Son and Holy Spirit are by your side as you walk by faith and not by sight. Imagine walking in a strange land all alone with no support or not knowing that a greater Authority is backing you up? It can be a scary thought to have to process but, on the other hand, knowing that you are cared for makes everything worth the journey. May God bless and keep you always. You will make it by the grace of God. Amen.

About The Author

Rosita Pinder is a woman who loves the Lord and has been serving him from her teenage years. She has a passion for writing and seeing the lives of others transformed for the better.

She believes in Habakkuk 2:2-3 (KJV), "2 And the LORD answered me, and said, Write the vision, and make it plain upon tables, that he may run that readeth it. 3 For the vision is yet for an appointed time, but at the end it shall speak, and not lie: though it tarry, wait for it; because it will surely come, it will not tarry." When the vision is written down, it is the first step to bringing your dream to reality.

Through the changing seasons in life her reliance has always been on minimising the outside noise and listening to the small inner voice, which ignites hope, joy and peace. She loves to exercise, hike and embrace the beauty of nature and in cooking healthy dishes to share with her family and friends. Giving is my nature and I hope to one day do so by establishing a charity to help young women with

self-esteem and self-worth workshops to empower
and to give back from the many intangible blessings
of God in her life.